A TOUR OF THE MOURNES

To the memory of Estyn Evans, 1905-1989

The publication has received support from the Cultural Traditions Group of the Community Relations Council.

The Friar's Bush Press
24 College Park Avenue
Belfast BT7 1LR
Published 1991

ISBN 0 946872 47 3

Designed by Rodney Miller Associates, Belfast
Printed by W. & G. Baird, Antrim

The Photographs
Front cover: Deer's Meadow (WAG 1723)
Back cover: W.A. Green on the Carginagh Road, near Kilkeel (WAG 571)

The WAG numbers after each photograph refer to the Green Collection held at the Ulster Folk and Transport Museum, Cultra, Co. Down, from where prints may be obtained.

A Tour
of the
Mournes

Historic Photographs of south-east Down
from the W. A. Green Collection
at the Ulster Folk and Transport Museum.

Fred Hamond and Tom Porter

FRIAR'S BUSH PRESS

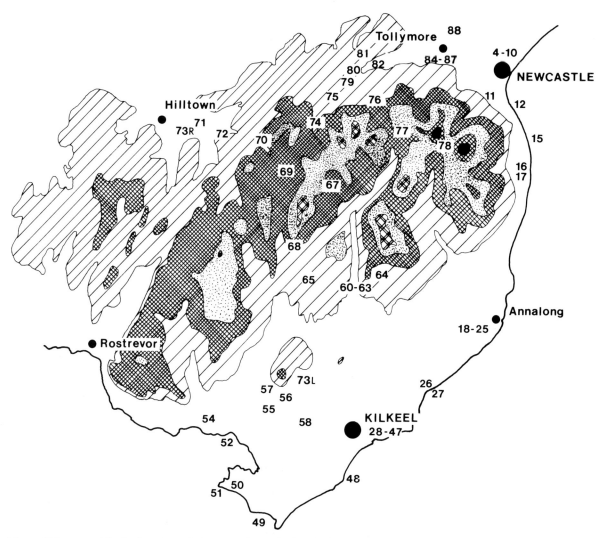

Map of Mourne with the location of photographs in the book identified by page.

INTRODUCTION

Although of comparatively small extent, the Mournes are not only one of Ireland's most striking mountain ranges, but probably also its best known, thanks to Percy French and his unforgettable song. The granite massif stretches some 15 miles from Newcastle to Rostrevor, "sweeping down to the sea" at both places. Most of the peaks exceed 1500ft, the highest being Slieve Donard, at 2796ft. Between the hills and the sea is the Kingdom of Mourne, a fertile agricultural region served by Kilkeel, Annalong and Ballymartin.

The mountains were formed some 50 million years ago when lava poured into a subterranean cavity in the Silurian bedrock which covered south-east Ulster. The overburden was subsequently weathered to expose the granite which had formed as the lava cooled. Final shaping of the peaks and valleys then took place over several Ice Ages.

With the final retreat of the ice some 10,000 years ago, trees colonized the area, even up to the highest peaks.[1] It was a productive environment for Mesolithic hunters, some of whose remains have recently been discovered.[2] Around 5000 years ago, farming communities settled in the area, attracted by the light fertile soils. They left behind megalithic tombs, the most prominent of which are the cairns on Slieve Donard.[3]

Early Christian literature, post-500AD, makes the first reference to the area, calling it *Boirche*, ('high place' or 'mountainous district'). The area was then populated by various clans and septs, some of whom lived in raths (small farmsteads surrounded by an earthen bank and ditch), many of which still survive. It was unlikely, however, that the area was a kingdom in its proper sense, as the Downpatrick-based *Dal Fiatach* then held sway over the area.

Mourne came under Norman influence in the 13th century, as evidenced by the castles of Carlingford, Greencastle, and Dundrum. It is around this time that we find the first references to 'Mourne', a name said to stem from Cremourne in Co. Monaghan, from whence the Mughdorna clan came to settle the area.

In 1552 Mourne was granted to Nicholas Bagnal. In 1715 it was inherited by Robert Needham, passing to his namesake in 1806. It was the latter, created first Earl of Kilmorey in 1832, who built Mourne Park, the Kingdom's only 'big house'.

Until the early 1800s, the area's only connection with the outside world was by sea, and along the coast to Newcastle and Newry. Even with the construction of a third highway through the mountains, the coastal lowlands remained a place apart until comparatively recently. It is this isolation which has given the area its resemblance to a kingdom, and which is still reflected in the many surnames peculiar to the area.[4]

Agriculture was, and is, the area's foremost industry. Arable cultivation focused on oats, barley, flax, and potatoes, and animal husbandry on cattle, pigs and sheep, the last being especially suited to the harsh upland environment.

Herring fishing was an important adjunct to subsistence farming. During the the later 1800s it was to develop as a major industry in its own right, focused on Annalong and Kilkeel.

The mountains themselves provided two important resources - granite and water. Thousands of tons of dressed granite were exported to Britain in the 1800s and early 1900s, mainly for street paving. For many decades the Silent Valley and Spelga reservoirs have supplied Belfast and the Co. Down lowlands with drinking water.

It was the grandeur of the mountains which captured the outside world's imagination, and as early as 1837 adventurous ladies were ascending Slieve Donard.[5] Over succeeding decades many writers extolled the area's merits, notably Robert Praeger in his *Official Guide to County Down and the Mourne Mountains*, published in 1898.[6]

The Belfast & Co. Down Railway Company (BCDR), was instrumental in developing tourism in Mourne. Based at the company's Slieve Donard Hotel, visitors could explore the many by-ways of Mourne, both high and low, on foot, bicycle and horse-drawn car.

The photographer, William Alfred Green (1870-1958), was one such visitor. He travelled throughout the area in his Model-T Ford between 1915 and 1940,[7] He had set up in Belfast as a professional in 1910, having served his apprenticeship with R. J. Welch, the Province's leading photographer.

Green's photographs are of interest in two respects. First, they show many aspects of Mourne which survived up to the recent past, but which have now been swamped by 'progress'. Perhaps more significantly, they also show the traditional granite and fishing industries at a time when both were on the wane, and prior to their restructuring in the 1930s. They therefore show Mourne at a time before a time.

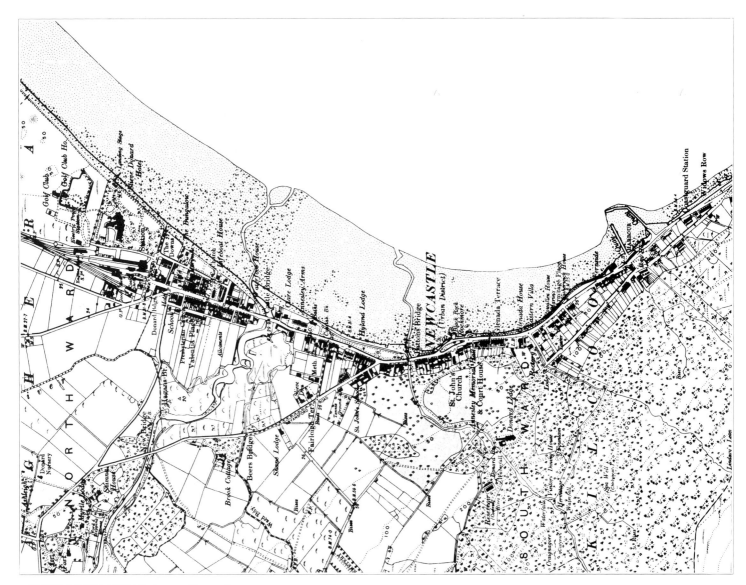

NEWCASTLE, 1920 (Ordnance Survey)

2

NEWCASTLE

For most people, Newcastle is the gateway to the Mournes. Its name derives from a tower house erected by Felix Magennis in 1588 at the mouth of the Shimna River, on the site of an earlier castle.

In 1747 the castle and surrounding lands were purchased by William Annesley of Castlewellan. In 1831, his successor, the 3rd Earl Annesley, built Donard Lodge as a summer residence on Thomas's Mountain and commenced planting the slopes with trees. Then Newcastle was but a small village at what is now the harbour end of town. Its population, then numbering fewer than 1000, was mainly engaged in farming, fishing and quarrying.

During the 1830s, Lord Annesley started developing Newcastle as a seaside resort. He opened the Annesley Arms Hotel and a bath house on the site of Magennis's castle, and by 1845 the town was being described as *'the queen of northern bathing places'*.[8]

The Annesley Estate also instigated extensive harbour improvements in the 1820s, and again in the 1850s. This greatly facilitated the export of agricultural produce, and also granite, drawn on a funicular railway from quarries on Thomas's Mountain.

Substantial two-storey villas and terraces began to spring up in the area between the harbour and Annesley Arms, and to the north of the Shimna. Gradually, the small fishing village was turning into a medium-sized seaside resort.

This transformation received a boost with the extension of the Belfast-Downpatrick railway to Newcastle in 1869. Newcastle, with its memorable combination of sand, sea and spectacular mountain backdrop, was now accessible to thousands in the rapidly expanding industrial town of Belfast. Not surprisingly the resort blossomed. In the 1890s alone, its permanent population increased by 50% to almost 1500, a growth unsurpassed in Mourne.

The town's reputation as one of Ireland's premier resorts was confirmed with the opening of the opulent Slieve Donard Hotel in 1898. This was built by the BCDR at a cost of almost £90,000 - some £15 million in today's terms.

At the time of Green's visits, Newcastle was spreading westwards along the Shimna and Bryansford Roads, a process which has continued northwards in the post-war years. However if one compares his views with the same scenes today, the Victorian and Edwardian building stock has survived remarkably intact behind the modern shop fronts.

Saturday Half Holiday
EXCURSION
TO
NEWCASTLE
By Excursion Express Train.
GOING.

Belfast	dep.	...	1- 0 p.m.
Newcastle	arr.	...	2-10 ,,

RETURNING.

Newcastle	dep.	...	8- 5 p.m
Belfast	arr.	...	9-15 ,,

Belfast to Newcastle and Back :

1st Class	2nd Class	3rd Class
3/-	2/6	2/-

NO LUGGAGE ALLOWED.

Available for return on date of issue only.

A summer special of 1892 run by the BCDR.

NEWCASTLE FROM THE SLIEVE DONARD HOTEL (WAG 3A)
The town is dominated by the granite mass of Slieve Donard, named after St Domangard, a disciple of St Patrick, who had a hermitage in one of the summit cairns. To the right of the distinctive ice-cut saddle is Slieve Commedagh (2515ft). A granite quarry is all too evident on the slopes of Thomas's Mountain at the left. Nestling in the trees below is Lord Annesley's Donard Lodge (demolished in 1966). The National Trust has recently purchased a large tract of the mountainside.

NEWCASTLE RAILWAY STATION (WAG 3484)

The station was built by the BCDR in 1905 to replace a more modest building of 1869. [9] From 1906, it was also the terminus of the Banbridge-Castlwellan line, operated jointly with the Great Northern Railway. The building is dominated by the huge clock tower and ornate glazed portico, outside which the jaunting cars, licenced to operate within a four mile radius, await the early morning train. The line closed in 1950, and the station now houses a shopping complex.

SLIEVE DONARD HOTEL (WAG 3112)
This imposing hotel was built by the BCDR at a cost of £44,000, with the furnishings costing almost as much again. Opening in 1898, it boasted 120 bedrooms, therapeutic baths, recreation rooms, electric lights and telephones. To stimulate custom, the BCDR offered inclusive rail-hotel packages from Belfast. Recently refurbished, it continues to function as one of the province's leading hotels.

ROYAL CO. DOWN GOLF CLUB (WAG 3115)

In 1889 the Co. Down Golf Club was founded by a group of prominent Belfast businessmen, and a links created on the dunes north of the station. The clubhouse was then a small shed on the platform. In 1897 a purpose-built clubhouse was opened, partly financed by the BCDR. A golfers' express ran on Saturdays from Belfast. Guests at the Slieve Donard Hotel could also play the links. In 1908, the club became the 'Royal', and has since hosted many championships. 10 The 60ft chimney (centre), now gone, was linked to the Slieve Donard's steam-powered electricity generator.

MAIN STREET, NEWCASTLE (WAG 566)

Much of Main Street's frontage dates to the 1880s and '90s. On the right is the Donard Hotel, Newcastle Presbyterian Church, and Anglesea Terrace. At foreground left is Nugent's hairdressers, with St Mary's spire in the background. Street lighting was provided by electricity generators in Donard Park. The scene is largely unchanged to this day (even the hairdresser's is still there), although the jaunting car has given way to one-way motor traffic.

THE PROMENADE, NEWCASTLE (WAG 567)

The laying out of the promenade was financed by Lord Annesley in the 1890s. At centre is the bandstand erected in 1905, and home to many seasons of entertaining pierrots. To the left is St John's Church of Ireland church , opened in 1832, and with late Victorian terraces to the right. In 1987, the bandstand was re-erected at Rowallane (Saintfield); only the plinth now remains in situ. In 1951, a granite fountain at the south end of the Promenade was dedicated to the memory of Percy French (1854-1920), author of 'Where the Mountains of Mourne sweep down to the sea.'[11]

CASTLE PARK, 1930s (WAG 3092)
Castle Park lies immediately upstream of Castle Bridge, and both recall Magennis's 16th century tower house. Here the Shimna River is dammed to form a recreational boating lake. Behind it are the twin Shimna Road bridges, erected when the street was laid out around 1930. A new town library has recently been erected at foreground right.

DONARD FALLS, NEWCASTLE (WAG 2621A)

Descending 1500ft from Slieve Commedagh to the sea, the Glen River is arguably the most spectacular of all Mourne's rivers. Over its two mile course, it tumbles over numerous waterfalls, as here at Donard Falls, near Donard Lodge. In the 1920s, the river was harnessed to generate electricity for the town's lighting. In the late 1800s, the Annesley Estate began abstracting water for the town. Only recently has this supply been superseded by the Silent Valley.

NEWCASTLE HARBOUR (WAG 2723A)

The harbour dates to the 1820s, and was substantially rebuilt and extended in 1850. It was then home to a large inshore fishing fleet, and to H. M. Coastguard from the later 1800s. On the quayside, granite kerbstones from nearby quarries await shipment. King Street, the focus of the old fishing village, overlooks the harbour in the background. At its south end, out of shot, is Widows' Row, built by public subscription to house the dependents of the 46 Newcastle fishermen who lost their lives in the fishing disaster of 1843.

NEWCASTLE FISHWIVES (WAG 278)
A wide variety of fish was caught along the coast, although herring and mackerel predominated. Whilst most was destined for British markets, some was sold locally. Itinerant dealers, known as 'cadgers', hawked the fish around the countryside. Here, three fishwives pose with their baskets of plaice.

13

BRINGING HOME THE 'TATTIES' NEAR NEWCASTLE (WAG 272)

Two boys, complete with Eton-type collars, are seen carrying potatoes and whins in creels. Mourne was, and is, a major producer of potatoes. Whins (elsewhere called gorse) were bruised on stones and fed to livestock; now unused, the bushes give vivid colour to the landscape when in blossom. This photograph is obviously posed as such creels were seldom used in Mourne during the present century. It is also doubtful whether the boy on the left could have walked far with such a weight of spuds.

MAGGIE'S LEAP (WAG 36)

The granite mountains are ringed by Silurian shales, cut into by numerous igneous dykes. Here at Maggie's Leap, the dyke itself has been eroded away, leaving a chasm some 100ft deep by 10ft wide. It is reputedly named after Maggie Murphy, a local girl who, whilst carrying a basket of eggs, jumped the gap to escape the attentions of an unwanted suitor. Both the girl and the eggs apparently survived. St Patrick's Stream, which marks the northern boundary of the Kingdom of Mourne, flows nearby.

BLOODY BRIDGE (WAG 18)

This old bridge stands a short distance upstream of the present road bridge. The stream which flows underneath was formerly called the Midpace River, but was renamed after a massacre during the 1641 Rebellion. Seemingly a group of prisoners, variously estimated to number between 10 and 50, was en route from Newry to Downpatrick, to be exchanged for rebel prisoners. Russell, the commander of the insurgents, fearing a double-cross, slew his captives at this spot. Afterwards, the stream is said to have run red for two days.[12]

ST MARY'S CHURCH, BLOODY BRIDGE (WAG 14)

Just south of the bridge is St Mary's, also known as Kilnahatin (church of the whins). It is cited in a document of 1615, but is probably earlier, and was under the jurisdiction of St Colman's, Kilkeel.[13] The arch between the nave and chancel is a masterpiece of construction, springing from dressed granite abutments. To this day it survives as shown here, and has apparently done so since at least 1845. Its locality, Ballaghanery, signifies 'the pass of the shepherd'.

NEWCASTLE ROAD, ANNALONG, *c*.1915 (WAG 1799)

Two Norton & Shaw vehicles stand outside the pub of their Annalong agent J. Gibney. The leading vehicle is a 'long car', with a capacity of 10-12 passengers, and used on scheduled passenger services between Newcastle and Kilkeel. The following vehicle is a 'tourist car', capable of carrying up to 16 front-facing sightseers. Such cars were superseded by motor buses after World War I.

ANNALONG

Annalong, sometimes also known as Islealong, lies midway between Newcastle and Kilkeel. Until the opening of Kilkeel Harbour in the 1870s, it was the only port of any significance along the entire Mourne coast between Carlingford and Newcastle. Its name denotes the 'ford of the ships', reflecting its situation at the mouth of the Annalong River which here cuts through the rocky foreshore to the sea. Small fishing boats could thus gain the sheltered creek behind, and it was around it that a hamlet of fishermen's houses evolved during the 1600s.

A map of 1822 shows that a small dock had, by then, been excavated on the south side of the river, opposite the cornmill. In the 1840s, and again in the 1880s, improvements were made to the dock, the entrance channel deepened, and quays and piers added.[14]

Annalong was an important fishing port, herring, mackerel, and haddock being the principal catches. In the summer of 1883 alone, almost 100 boats discharged £10,000 worth of fish - £2 million in today's terms. Many of the fishermen were part-timers, farming being their mainstay. Traditionally, they employed drift nets and long-lines. The latter involved suspending hundreds of baited hooks from an anchored line up to half a mile deep. The catch was divided up on a 'share' basis: the owner received half the net proceeds, with the rest being split between skipper and crew. The catch was sold fresh, or salted in wooden barrels. Since the early 1900s, herring have also been smoked in a kippering store adjacent to the harbour.

Annalong was also a major trading port. By the early 1800s, it was already engaged in the export of granite and potatoes to Belfast and Britain, and the importation of coal – commodities which were to remain its mainstay over the next century.

Although a hard durable stone, granite is relatively easy to split and dress into blocks on account of its grain or 'rede'. It was widely used locally for buildings and headstones. Vast quantities were also exported as kerbstones (cribben) and squared cobblestones (setts). Much of the granite was derived from surface scatters of boulders on the east-facing mountain slopes between Slieve Bingian and Bloody Bridge. It was worked by farmers to augment their meagre incomes, and transported to the Annalong stone merchants on horse-drawn carts.[15] This activity, along with fishing, greatly alleviated the worst effects of the Famine in the 1840s.

The industry's heyday was in the later 1800s, when tens of thousands of tons were exported annually to Belfast and Lancashire, where miles of surfaced road were being laid out. By the early 1900s,

however, it was in decline, due to the increasing use of tarmac and concrete. The First World War saw trade decline to almost zero, and it was but a pale shadow of its former self thereafter.

In the inter-war years, the granite merchants switched their attention to monumental masonry. This required larger blocks of stone, only obtainable from deep quarries, such as those on Slieve Bingian, Seefin, and Chimney Rock. With the cessation of foreign imports during the Second World War, increased reliance on indigenous stone gave a fillip to the industry. Improved lorry transport, and the electrical mechanization of cutting, dressing and polishing, also led to a shift in operations from the quarries to Annalong itself. Two stone yards remain at work today.

Until the last war, Annalong remained a small village of less than 300 people. In recent years it has expanded greatly, and its population is fast approaching 2000. No maritime trade is now carried on, and the fishing fleet is based at Kilkeel. However, small skiffs continue to set out for inshore waters each autumn to harvest the herring.[16] Much of the catch is still kippered at the harbour, whilst a modern factory on the Moneydarragh Road processes shellfish.

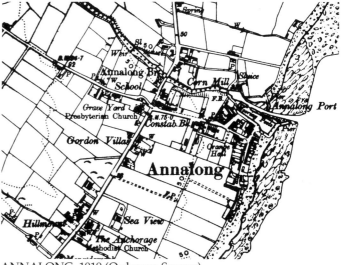

ANNALONG, 1919 (Ordnance Survey)

19

NEWCASTLE ROAD, ANNALONG, *c.*1930 (WAG 2720)
A still-familiar view of the village from the Newcastle approach. To the left are various buildings associated with Hamilton's granite yard, behind which the road crosses the Annalong River.

At top right is Annalong Presbyterian Church, devoid of its modern tower. Although the telephone had arrived, electricity did not come until the 1930s.

MAIN STREET, ANNALONG, *c.*1930 (WAG 2720B)
Gordon's stone yard is at centre right, with Robinson's opposite. The stone was hand-dressed in the row of small sheds, most of the output being exported from the harbour. Robinson's yard now uses mechanized equipment, and local granite has been usurped by a variety of foreign imports, used mainly for monumental purposes.

ANNALONG HARBOUR, *c.*1915 (WAG 1797)

Being a major trading port, Annalong was home to many schooners and skiffs. On the quayside, granite and potatoes await export. To the left is Gordon's pub (now the Harbour Inn). Incoming boats lined up with the navigation mark at the back of the harbour. To the right is the water-powered Annalong cornmill, built around 1800. In the early 1900s, a steam engine and chimney were added when the Annalong River was tapped for the Belfast water supply.

ANNALONG HARBOUR, *c*.1930 (WAG 2688)

The same view some 15 years on. Motor-powered boats, such as the foreground skiff, are now appearing. On the left, the S.S. *Jolly Frank* is discharging material for the Silent Valley Reservoir, then under construction. It was conveyed to the Valley along a purpose-built railway (dismantled when the reservoir opened).

At the mill, the steam engine has been replaced by an oil engine, the cooling tanks of which are above the waterwheel. The mill, which ran until the 1960s, is now part of the Newry and Mourne District Council's marine park, and is fully working.[17]

ANNALONG FROM SCHOOL ROAD, *c.*1915 (WAG 1796)
Although slates were imported into Annalong from the early 1800s, some one-storey cottages remained thatched. The foreground house has rope thatch, held secure to projecting spikes on the eaves and gables.[18] To the right, the main Newcastle - Kilkeel Road crosses the Annalong River. On the far bank, the mill race from the nearby 'battery' (weir) to the cornmill is just visible. Hamilton's stone yard is at centre right.

ANNALONG FROM SCHOOL ROAD, *c*.1940 (WAG 2737)
Some 25 years on from the previous view, and Annalong is
beginning to expand, with the erection of a small estate of hip-
roofed houses by Kilkeel Rural District Council in 1937
(background right). The semi-detached houses to their left were
built for veterans of World War I. The two cottages below them,
formerly thatched, are now slated. Beside them (at centre) is one
of Hamilton's lorries which brought the stone from the quarries.
In recent decades the Housing Executive has built a large number
of houses at this end of Annalong.

BALLYMARTIN (WAG 1854)

The village straggles along the main coast road midway between Annalong and Kilkeel. St Patrick's Catholic Church, built in 1825 on the site of an earlier church, is prominent on the left. Behind the cart at the centre of the picture is a one-storey blacksmith's shop which operated until the 1960s. Opposite it is a steam-powered road tractor belonging to the BCDR. The company ran a daily freight service between Newcastle and Kilkeel from 1905 to the 1930s.

FISHERMAN'S COTTAGE, BALLYMARTIN GLEN (WAG 1196)

Fishing was an important adjunct to farming and the coastal inlets and dykes provided ideal landing places for small boats. This cabin is one of several along the shore in the vicinity of Mahula's Well. The rope-thatched roof (with oar) was designed to withstand the strong east winds. Its single room is of the 'direct-entry' type, the door being at the opposite end to the hearth. Only its foundations now survive, whilst the adjacent cottages are now week-end retreats.

COTTAGE NEAR KILKEEL (WAG 2679)

This cottage, on the Kilkeel River above the harbour, differs in two respects from the Ballymartin example (page 27). The roof has scallop thatch, in which the bundles of straw are secured with briar 'staples'; rope thatch is, however, more usual hereabouts. There is also a second room beyond the chimney, a feature typical of Mourne, but less so elsewhere. Surrounding the house are numerous stone 'ditches', ubiquitous throughout the region. This particular locality has recently been relandscaped, and nothing of the cottage survives.

CRAWTREE STONE, KILKEEL (WAG 588)

At the end of the last Ice Age, the retreating glaciers left large erratics along their paths. Some later found use as prehistoric burial chambers, as here on the northern outskirts of Kilkeel. Erected by farmers some 5000 years ago, the megalith (variously called a portal tomb, dolmen, giant's grave or cromlech) probably contained the remains of the community's more important members, and would originally have been covered with a cairn of stones.

MOURNE DRILL PLOUGH (WAG 1978)

The relatively light soils of Mourne were easily worked into raised drills. The drill plough comprises an almost-symmetrical wooden mould board which buried the seed potato by pushing the loose soil up on either side as it was pulled along. It could be easily adapted to conventional cutting and turning of the soil by removing one of the mould boards and adding a coulter. Such ploughs were seldom found outside Mourne.[19]

BINGING POTATOES (WAG 280)

When harvested in the autumn, potatoes were usually stored in bings (clamps). The heaped-up potatoes were covered with 'sprit' (sedge grass) and 'happed' with a protective layer of well compacted soil. In this way the potatoes remained fresh over the winter and spring. With modern storage methods, the practice has now all but died out. The export of seed potato is still an important facet of Mourne agriculture. Eelworm has, however, forced potato growers to rent fields elsewhere in the county.

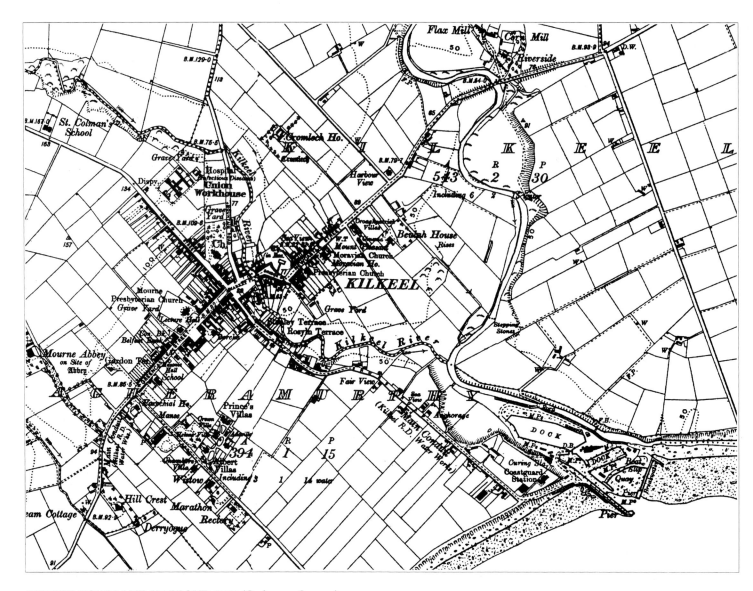

KILKEEL TOWN AND HARBOUR, 1919 (Ordnance Survey)

KILKEEL

Kilkeel is the principal town of the Kingdom of Mourne. Its name signifies 'the church of the narrows', referring to the old Parish Church of St Colman, the ruins of which still stand above the Aughrim River, half a mile from the coast.

Some contend the church was founded by St Colman in the 5th century. Others say it was built by a Spanish nobleman in gratitude to the people of Kilkeel for burying his son, drowned off the Mourne coast. Whatever the truth, documents confirm a church on this spot from the 1300s. Indeed, the large circular earthwork which surrounds the graveyard suggests an even earlier existence.

The nearby Crawtree Stone (page 29) and several Early Christian 'forths' (raths) indicate that farming communities were present in the area since around 3000BC. However, it was in the vicinity of the church that the present-day town gradually developed.

Whilst Kilkeel was always the ecclesiastical focus of Mourne, it was not until the demise of Greencastle in the 1600s that it also became its administrative capital. By the early 1800s it was a flourishing town, engaged in small-scale industry, trade and commerce.[20] This period saw the construction of many substantial two-storey houses, and public buildings such as the courthouse (with market house below), Kilmorey Arms Hotel, and Christ Church.

Prior to the Famine, Kilkeel was broadly similar in both in size and population to Newcastle.[21] The Famine did not unduly hinder its development, although it was necessary to open a workhouse in 1841.[22] However, despite the proximity of a long strand along Kilkeel bay and nearby Cranfield beach, Kilkeel could never match Newcastle as a seaside resort. Rather, it was to develop in a quite different way - as the Kingdom's principal market town and fishing port.[23] With a population now in excess of 6000, these twin roles are still very much to the fore today.

It is perhaps now hard to imagine that for three-quarters of the 19th century, Annalong boasted a far superior port. At Kilkeel, the fishermen were forced to beach their craft on the open shore and at nearby Derryogue, as a long gravel spit at the mouth of the Kilkeel River hindered the building of a harbour.

It was not until 1868 that the bar was breached and a small pier erected south of the river. This was followed, in 1873, by a dock capable of holding 20 vessels.

Kilkeel proved a particularly convenient location to land catches, and quickly attracted boats from all over the British Isles. Quayside activity focused on the processing of herring and mackerel, destined mainly for the English market. Growth was such that a boat building yard and herring smokery were both set up in the 1870s, and it was also during this decade that Kilkeel supplanted Annalong in importance as a fishing port.

Although the harbour quickly became congested, it was not until 1887 that the basin was deepened and quayage developed immediately east of the dock.

In 1890 alone, more than one third of all herring landed in Ireland came through Kilkeel. However, the first decades of the present century brought recession, compounded by the fact that steamers now brought in cargoes which earlier had been carried by locally-based schooners.[24]

The war itself brought a brief revival of fortunes, and the building of a large inner dock to the west of the existing complex.

The continuing demise of the industry was reversed by the inception of 'seine' netting around 1930. Unlike traditional long-line and drift-net techniques, used for surface-feeding herring shoals, the net was pulled along near the sea bed, thus catching bottom feeders such as whiting, cod, sole and plaice.

This technique was only made possible by the use of motorized boats, more powerful than any sail-assisted vessel. It was just before the outbreak of the First World War that Lord Kilmorey had brought the first motorized boat, the *Ellen Constance*, into Kilkeel, having purchased it in Lowestoft. By the late thirties most boats had been motorized and equipped with seine nets.

The 1970s saw a substantial extension of the harbour to the west, and the diversion of the river into its upper end.

Now with over 100 boats, ranging from small skiffs to deep-sea trawlers worth over £2 million, Kilkeel boasts the largest fishing fleet in Ireland. Its harbour is a hive of industry with fish processing factories, a marine engineer's, ice factory, fish market, and ship repair works. In all, the industry gives employment to some 1500 people.

Green's photographs show the harbour after its Great War improvements, but before sail had given way to steam. His town views also show that, despite today's proliferation of plastic shop fronts, the town's inner core has remained surprisingly intact.

KILKEEL FROM THE SOUTH-EAST (WAG 587)
This unusual view, taken near the graveyard of Kilkeel
Presbyterian Church, shows the rear of Bridge Street above the
Aughrim River. The picture is dominated by Christ Church
(C. of I.), built in 1815 with later additions. Inside, plaques
commemorate the Kilmoreys, and also General F.R. Chesney,
'father of the Suez Canal'.[25] On the extreme right is part of the
Royal Hotel which is now in ruins.

BRIDGE STREET, KILKEEL (WAG 596)

Looking south from the Newcastle end, various commercial and domestic premises come into view. Of note is the building to the right of Green's car; a datestone over the right-hand arch commemorates its building (as an inn) by J. Shannon in 1818.

The steps at the right lead into the old St Colman's Church. In 1815 it was superseded by Christ Church (centre picture), but continued in use as a school until the turn of the century.

THE SQUARE, LOOKING TOWARDS NEWRY STREET,
KILKEEL (WAG 593)

The Square is the meeting point of roads from Newcastle, Newry, Greencastle and the harbour. The famous granite steps, a point of popular congregation, are seen on the left. For many years, fairs have been held hereabouts on the last Wednesday of every month. Those in April and November are still the biggest, even though the payment of rent on a half-yearly basis has ceased. Randall's pub has now been rebuilt as the Lantern Bar. The corner building on the left has recently been removed and the steps set back to ease traffic congestion.

GREENCASTLE STREET FROM THE SQUARE,
KILKEEL (WAG 594)

Since the early 1800s, Greencastle Street has been the commercial artery of the town. Further up the street, just out of shot, is Mourne Presbyterian Church, Kilmorey Arms Hotel, and the now-demolished court and market house. Note the large trailer, left of centre, used by the BCDR in connection with their freight service to Newcastle (*cf.* page 26). The building on the right has now been raised to three storeys.

MRS RYAN'S SEACLIFFE TEA-ROOMS, KILKEEL (WAG 2993)
Located near the junction of the Esplanade and Manse Road, this was a popular venue with both locals and visitors in the 1920s and 1930s. Although the tea-rooms have long since closed, the buildings continue in use as private dwellings.

THE GLEN, KILKEEL (WAG 592)
Situated between the Manse Road and Derryogue Harbour, this narrow track down to the shore was once a favourite walk for townsfolk. Although now somewhat neglected, the path can still be walked.

KILKEEL HARBOUR, FROM THE WEST (WAG 1724)
Schooners and fishing boats lie side by side, whilst materials await handling on the quayside to the left. Note the outer pier, and the bottleneck created by the narrow entrance to the harbour proper. The store in the centre foreground has long since been removed.

KILKEEL HARBOUR, FROM THE EAST (WAG 2677)
Looking towards the inner basin, with the Kilkeel River in the foreground. Many of the smaller fishing boats were beached at the top end. With the westward extension of the basin in the 1970s, the river was diverted into its top end and the stream bed hereabouts infilled. A large fish market now occupies the area to the right. The track at the bottom right leads off to Moor Road.

THE DOCK, KILKEEL HARBOUR, FROM THE SOUTH-WEST
(WAG 598)

The boats are tightly packed, it being a Sunday when none were at work. Fish barrels litter the quayside at the left, whilst cribben awaits shipment to the right. In the last century the fishing boats often doubled as coasters to carry granite and potatoes to Britain.

Although the *Millbay* at the bottom right was registered in Plymouth, it was probably locally owned. A large boat repair slip now occupies the far end of the dock.

DOCK AND COASTGUARD STATION, FROM THE NORTH-EAST (WAG 2683)

The view looking the opposite way to the previous page, shows the imposing coastguard station overlooking the harbour. This red-brick two-storey terrace was built *c.*1904, and replaced an earlier station at nearby Leestone Point. Each of its five houses would have accommodated a man and his family; there is also a small look-out on the gable at the harbour end. The complex has has recently been sold off for private development.

QUAYSIDE, KILKEEL HARBOUR (WAG 599)
As today, people turned out in their Sunday best for a stroll around the harbour when the fleet was berthed (*cf.* page 42). Here the boats are tied up along the quay at the harbour entrance.

Immediately to the right of the house on the left is the louvred ridge ventilator of the kippering store.

KIPPERING STORE, KILKEEL HARBOUR (WAG 3381)
The first fish smokery was established at the harbour in the 1870s by Donald Stewart of Newry. Gutted herrings were suspended over smouldering oak shavings, so imparting a distinctive flavour to the curing fish. The rate of burning was controlled by adjusting the roof shutters. In 1924 a Kilkeel kipper won a first prize at the Wembley Food Exhibition. The building survives, albeit no longer in original use. A similar smokery still operates at Annalong Harbour.

BOAT YARD, KILKEEL HARBOUR (WAG 600)

In 1875, a Cornishman, William Paynter, set up a boat yard at the mouth of the Kilkeel River. Its water turned a wheel which supplied motive power to the works. Although he revolutionized local boat design, his venture was not altogether successful, and he sold out to John Mackintosh in 1883. His son, also John, was running the business when this picture was taken. The building was demolished c.1970. However, repair work to boats continues on the slipway at the nearby dock. John Kearney maintains the tradition of hand-crafted boat building at Annalong.

FISHING BOATS (WAG 1983)

Lug-sailed yawls set out to the fishing grounds. The autumn was a particularly bountiful period, as herring shoals then came close to shore. Various coastal landmarks enabled the boats to locate their position. Although most of the fleet is now geared to deep-sea fishing, motorized skiffs from Kilkeel and Annalong continue to harvest the inshore herring in September and October, the waters becoming alive with bobbing lights as darkness falls.

KILKEEL BAY, FROM THE SOUTH (WAG 2680)
The bay sweeps north from Derryogue Harbour to Leestone
Point; the Kilkeel coastguard station is prominent at the centre. In
contrast to the rocky shoreline elsewhere in Mourne, the coast
here comprises slowly-eroding cliffs of sand and gravel,
deposited during the last Ice Age. Although making up the most
fertile land in the Kingdom, the deposits have been extensively
quarried in many parts of the Cranfield Peninsula. Nearby is the
former Greencastle Aerodrome, used by the American Air Force
during the last war.[26]

CRANFIELD BAY (WAG 2987)
A southerly aspect and sandy beach make Cranfield a popular summer resort. There was a golf course on the dunes at the right until the late 1940s. Thereafter, caravans appeared, and over the last ten years have entirely swamped the foreground area. Out of shot on the left is the Haulbowline lighthouse, built in 1823 to guide boats through the shallow mouth of Carlingford Lough to Greenore and Warrenpoint. In 1916 the S.S. *Connemara* collided with the *Retriever*, with the loss of 88 lives.

49

THE CASTLE, GREENCASTLE (WAG 46)

The castle was built in the mid-13th century, replacing a still-extant earthen motte to the west. Together with Carlingford Castle on the opposite shore, it commanded the narrow entrance to the lough. It was initially held by the de Burghs, Earls of Ulster. After an eventful history, it was granted to Sir Nicholas Bagnal in 1552, along with most of Mourne. The castle is now a state monument. Sadly gateposts such as those at foreground left are being increasingly replaced by nondescript concrete pillars.

GREENCASTLE (WAG 45)

At the western tip of the Cranfield peninsula is the hamlet of Greencastle. On the left is the coastguard station, built *c.*1877 to replace an earlier one near Cranfield Point. In 1884 the London & North Western Railway Co. built a pier to ferry people to Greenore, and so connect with their Holyhead and Liverpool ferries. This encouraged a substantial emigration from the area. A Norton & Shaw long car service connected with Kilkeel. However, a planned railway from Newcastle and Warrenpoint never materialized. The cross-channel service ceased in the 1920s.

MILL BAY (WAG 2718)

Seaweed ('wrack') makes an excellent fertilizer, particularly for potatoes. It was intensively cultivated on boulders laid out in lines on the broad inter-tidal flats of Mill Bay. Harvested in the spring, it was spread on fields throughout Mourne. In-blown weed ('tails') was also collected.[27] An excellent panorama of the wrack beds can be had from Knockshee (1144ft), shown in the centre of the picture; on its summit is a Bronze-Age cairn. Limestone was also quarried on an island just offshore, and burnt in nearby kilns for fertilizer.

DONKEY AND SEAWEED CREELS (WAG 274)

The seaweed was taken to the fields on carts and in creels. These light wooden contraptions had hinged bottoms which, when released, allowed the load to fall out. Little, if any, wrack was burnt for kelp, as was the case along the Antrim coast. Seaweed collection has now all but ceased in Mourne.

CASSY WATER ROAD-BRIDGE (WAG 2634)
This triple-arched bridge carries the main Kilkeel - Rostrevor road over the Cassy Water at the north end of Mill Bay. Also known as the Causeway Water, it marks the boundary of the Kingdom of Mourne with Lower Iveagh. Nearby is Kilfeaghan portal tomb, which, unlike the Crawtree Stone (page 29), still retains its cairn.

WHITE WATER ROAD-BRIDGE (WAG 2685)

No less than three bridges have carried the Kilkeel - Rostrevor road over the White Water at this point. The double-arched rubble-stone bridge seen here is probably of 18th century date. It was superseded in the early 1800s by a bridge to the south. In the 1960s, it too was replaced by today's structure. The original bridge survives in the grounds of Mourne Park, whilst the vicinity of its successor has been developed as an amenity area by Newry & Mourne District Council.

MOURNE PARK (WAG 2684)

In the early 1700s, the Mourne lands formerly belonging to Nicholas Bagnal passed to the Needhams. Around 1806 Robert Needham, later Lord Kilmorey, erected the present building at Mourne Park, on the site of an earlier house. The estate was also variously known as 'Ballyrogan', and 'Siberia'. This view shows the house from across the lake, with Knockchree (1015ft) behind. Various additions were made to the house by Needham's successors.

THE LADIES' POOL, MOURNE PARK (WAG 2996)
Flowing along the west side of Mourne Park, the White Water provided sport and relaxation for the Kilmoreys. Small weirs were erected across the river to create salmon pools, one of which was evidently also used for swimming. The demesne served as an army base during the Second World War. Latterly, part was given over to the Mourne Golf Club, previously at Cranfield (page 49). The woods are also used by scout groups for summer camps.

MOURNE GRANGE (WAG 2687)

Orginally known as Drumindoney, and of 19th century date, the house was leased to Allen Carey in 1900. He opened what was then Ireland's first preparatory school, Mourne Grange. Various extensions, including a chapel (shown right), were added over the next decade. Enrolment peaked at 104 around 1950.

Declining numbers forced the school's closure in 1971. The Mourne Grange Village Community then took over. Some 130 able-bodied and handicapped adults now live and work together, following principles advocated by Rudolf Steiner.

FLOWERING LINEN, KILKEEL (WAG 279)

Flax was an important cash crop in Mourne, and Kilkeel once boasted a thriving flax and brown linen market. Most of the flax was dispatched to mills outside the area for spinning, weaving and bleaching into white linen. Up until the Second World War, women and girls found home-based employment in hemming and flowering linen handkerchiefs distributed from the factories by local agents. Flowering involved the embroidery of designs in white and coloured thread, and required great skill and patience.

SILENT VALLEY (WAG 584)

The Silent Valley is one of the most picturesque areas in the Mournes. It was formerly also known as the Happy Valley. This photograph was taken prior to the construction of the reservoir in the 1920s. The effect of glaciation is clearly evident in the valley's U-shaped profile. The floor is infilled with glacial debris, through which runs the Kilkeel River. The slopes of Slievenaglogh are at the left, with Doan at the centre, and Bingian to the right. In the early 1900s, geese were grazed here, and walked to Dundrum for export to Whitehaven.

SILENT VALLEY (WAG 3600)

In 1901, the Kilkeel River was partly diverted along a pipeline around the east slopes of Slieve Bingian to join the Annalong River on a 35-mile journey to the Knockbracken reservoir at Carryduff. [28] Behind the diverting embankment, seen at the centre of the picture, is one of the many sand and gravel moraines left by the melting glaciers. Green evidently enhanced the flow of the river by judicious retouching.

WATER COMMISSIONERS' HOUSE, SILENT VALLEY
(WAG 585)

This view, looking north from just below the twin-arched Colligan Bridge, shows the house erected by the Belfast & District Water Commissioners in 1905 for the Valley superintendent. The Mourne Wall descends Slieve Bingian (centre). It was built between 1904 and 1922 to demarcate the Commissioners' 9000 acre catchment. The 6-8ft high dressed drystone wall is one of the wonders of Ireland, running for 22 miles over 15 mountain summits. It was the venue for an annual walk organized by the Youth Hostel Association between the mid-1950s and mid-1980s.

SILENT VALLEY RESERVOIR (WAG 2722)

The 500 yard dam was built between 1923 and 1933 at a cost of £1.35 million (now £70 million).[29] Some of the 2000-strong workforce lived on site, in a purpose-built village of tin-sheeted houses, a few of which still survive in the vicinity. The picture shows the overflow duct into the Kilkeel River. In 1952, the reservoir's 3000 million gallon capacity was augmented by the Annalong River, diverted through Slieve Bingian; the Ben Crom Reservoir was added in 1957. The Mourne scheme now supplies 30 million gallons per day to Greater Belfast area and much of Co. Down.

SLIEVE BINGIAN FROM THE EAST (WAG 1701)
At 2449ft, Slieve Bingian ('mountain of little peaks') dominates the south-eastern corner of Mourne. The Mourne Wall is again visible on the slopes of Wee Bingian (1509ft), at the left. Tracks lead up to quarries and numerous surface workings. The small farmstead at the centre was one of the highest in the Mournes, and is still used as a week-end cottage.

KILKEEL - HILLTOWN ROAD, NEAR CROCKNAFEOLA (WAG 2672)

Looking north, the road crosses the Yellow Water and heads up the valley between Pigeon Rock Mountain (left) and Slieve Muck (right). Turf awaits removal from the roadside to a nearby cottage. Just out of shot, right, lived a gamekeeper for the Kilmorey Estate; the house has only recently been demolished.

CARTING TURF (WAG 1973)
Upland peat bogs were extensively worked, as at the Castle and Red Bogs, north-east of Rostrevor. Lowland bogs also existed but were largely exhausted during the earlier 1800s. Slipes, solid-wheeled carts, and spoke-wheeled Scotch carts (shown here) were used to bring the dried turf home. Around the coast, coal was used in preference, being readily available through Annalong and Kilkeel. Now only the Red Bog remains in use, tractors and trailers drawing the turf away.

LOUGH SHANNAGH (WAG 1717)
The 'lake of the foxes' is the largest of Mourne's few natural lakes. Lying between Carn Mountain and Doan at 1400ft, it feeds into the Silent Valley some 900ft below. It is best approached along the Banns Road, a four-mile track off the main Hilltown road. In the late 1960s, a pumped-storage hydro-electric power scheme was proposed, but was abandoned on environmental grounds.[30]

GLACIAL ERRATIC, CROCKNAFEOLA (WAG 3609)

Most Mourne erratics are of granite, notably the Cloghmore Stone above Rostrevor. This example however, on the east side of the main road north of Crocknafeola Forest, is of Silurian rock, common throughout the rest of Co.Down. Many of the more accessible erratics have been quarried for building stone, or incorporated into prehistoric burial chambers, as at Kilfeaghan and Kilkeel (page 29).

DEER'S MEADOW (WAG 1723)

Surrounded by the high mountains of the Central Mournes, the Deer's Meadow has long been an important grazing ground. Sheep were valued for their wool and mutton, and the Blackface sheep shown here were well adapted to the upland conditions, harsh even in summer. Part of the Meadow and original mountain road are now under the Spelga Dam, opened in 1957; at times of low water, a bridge arch appears incongruously above the water line.

LOOKING DOWN THE SPELGA PASS (WAG 2671)

The Spelga Pass descends from the Deer's Meadow along the headwater of the River Bann to the Hilltown lowlands. In the 1700s and early 1800s, farmers and their families grazed cattle on the lush upland pastures over the summer months. Traces of their temporary 'booleys', their summer homes, can still be found east of Spelga Dam. This practice has long since ceased, but is recalled in Slievenamiskan (butter-tub mountain) and Butter Mountain. Although cattle are been driven along here, sheep are now the norm.

RIVER BANN EAST OF HILLTOWN (WAG 3060)

Green's photograph shows a heavily retouched stream quite unlike today's small trickle. The water of the Upper Bann was renowned for its softness and purity, and many bleach greens were established between Banbridge and Portadown in the 1700s. Nearby is Lough Island Reavy, which formerly also fed the Bann.

In 1839 it was embanked to form a huge millpond which ensured a steady flow of water over the summer months. A similar pond was proposed at the Deer's Meadow in the 1830s, but never implemented. Around 1980, a proposed reservoir at Kinnahalla was abandoned following a public inquiry.

COCK AND HEN MOUNTAINS (WAG 3062)
The twin peaks of Hen rise to 1189ft, with the 1666ft Cock Mountain behind. Why they should be thus called is unclear, as neither has any obvious resemblance. The torrent of water in the foreground is, in fact, a heavily retouched laneway.

WINNOWING CORN, LEITRIM HILL (WAG 277)
A farmer tosses threshed oats from a skin wight to separate the grain from the chaff. 'Shillin Hills', where this activity took place, are found in various parts of the Mourne.

WINDMILL NEAR HILLTOWN (WAG 1971)
This curious windmill is thought to have stood on a hillside east of Hilltown. Evidently a home-made device, four sails, affixed to a tree, drive two pulley wheels and a belt. The latter probably powered a roller for bruising corn. The means of adjusting the sails (to regulate their speed) is certainly novel, and reflects an ingenuity and pragmatism so often found in rural areas.

SLIEVENAMAN RESERVOIR (WAG 3054)
Also known as Fofanny Dam, this reservoir was built by the Portadown & Banbridge Regional Waterworks Joint Board in 1909 to supply the population of the Upper Bann Valley. Increasing demand eventually led to the construction of the nearby Spelga Dam in the 1950s. The water superintendent's house in the foreground right, has now been cleared, and the surrounding area planted with trees. In the background are (from left) Slieve Meelbeg, Slieve Loughshannagh, and Ott Mountain.

FARM ON SLIEVENAMAN (WAG 10)

Taken from the east slopes of Slievenaman, and with Hare's Gap in the background, this view shows a typical mountain farm. Unlike modern houses, the buildings are aligned along the slope to aid drainage. The complex is roofed with both slate and thatch, and would have incorporated a dwelling, byre and store. In the 'hagyard' are several hay stacks. The wall across the background slope defines the boundary between the lower sub-divided cultivated land and rough open moorland, suitable only for grazing.

HARE'S GAP (WAG 578)

A closer view of the Gap reveals its characteristic shape, the result of glacial downcutting during the last Ice Age. The valley floor between Slievenaglogh (left) and Bearnagh (right) is littered with glacial debris through which the Trassey River flows. In their heavy dress, it must have been hard going for Green's companions. From the top of the Gap, the Brandy Pad runs through the mountains to Bloody Bridge (page 16). This track takes its name from 18th century smuggling activity.

SLIEVE BEARNAGH FROM THE DIAMOND ROCKS
(WAG 581)

The walking party pauses for a rest at the Diamond Rocks on the south slopes of Slievenaglogh. The rocks take their name from quartz crystals which formed in small cavities in the granite as it cooled when intruded into the Silurian overburden. Such crystals are now difficult to find, thanks to the despoilations of countless amateur geologists. The distinctive summit tors of Bearnagh (2394ft) are just visible on the opposite side of the valley.

77

THE CASTLES OF KIVITAR (WAG 583)

Kivitar is the local name for Slieve Commedagh, which, at 2515ft, is the second highest mountain in the Mournes. The unusual castellated appearance of these tors, at the head of the Annalong Valley, is the result of thousands of years of weathering of horizontal and vertical joints within the granite, and are similar to those on Dartmoor.

SLIEVENAMAN YOUTH HOSTEL (WAG 3056)
To cater for walkers and climbers, the Youth Hostel Association ran hostels at Newcastle, Bloody Bridge, Silent Valley, Kinnahalla, and here at Slievenaman. The erection of this wooden chalet by volunteers in the 1930s was financed by the Crossgar Poultry Association. The Morrisons, who lived in the adjacent farmhouse, acted as wardens until the hostel's closure in 1981. Still retaining its distinctive green exterior, it is ironic that it is now a hen house, albeit partly collapsed. Now only the Newcastle hostel operates, supplemented by numerous outdoor field centres.

UPPER SHIMNA VALLEY (WAG 3058)

Viewed from the east slopes of Slievenaman, the Trassey River descends from the Hare's Gap between Clonachullion Hill (left) and the Spellack cliffs (right). The Trassey Bridge is clearly visible at the left and marks the start of the well-worn track (at the centre) up to the Gap. Behind Spellack, on the slopes of Slieve Bearnagh, is 'Clanwhillan' Quarry, now operated by Robinsons of Annalong, and one of the few still open in Mourne. It supplied granite for the seaward extension of the Newcastle Centre, a tourist amenity built in the 1980s by Down District Council.

UPPER SHIMNA VALLEY (WAG 573)

Kane's farm, at the centre, was one of the first in Mourne to have electricity, generated by water from the Trassey River between 1915 and 1978. At foreground left is the hump-backed Clonachullion Bridge over the Shimna. Clonachullion Hill, centre left, is now afforested, with the Ulster Way running along the wall at its base. A car park has recently been built where the path joins the road. It is dedicated to Cecil Newman who actively promoted environmental conservation in the Mournes.

FLAX SCUTCHING MILL, TULLYREE (WAG 1042)

Located just downstream of Clonachullion Bridge, this mill was erected about 1860 to separate flax fibre from the woody 'shous' which comprise the rest of the plant. Ten to fifteen people found employment here over the autumn and winter months. The waterwheel powered five scutching stocks and a set of rollers. When the Foffany Dam opened in 1909, water shortages became a problem. An engine was eventually installed in 1927, and the mill ran until the mid 1940s. Only fragments now remain.

HAMILTON'S FOLLY, TOLLYMORE (WAG 1831)
This folly marks the boundary of Tollymore Demesne, and was erected by the 2nd Lord Limerick, James Hamilton, in the late 1700s. The 'baps' – round stone protrusions – were a familiar feature of the estate architecture, and were inspired by Thomas Wright who had taught the young Hamilton mathematics in the 1740s. Gateposts of similar style can be seen behind Green's car. Further along, out of view, is another folly, and they are collectively known as Lord Limerick's Follies.

TOLLYMORE

In 1611, a number of townlands along the northern foothills of the Mournes were granted to Brian Magennis by James I. These included what is now Tollymore Demesne, the third landed estate, after Donard and Mourne Park, to impinge on our tour.

Tollymore signifies 'big hill', after the Drinns, the twin summits of which rise to 840ft on the southern boundary of the estate.

Around 1685, Tollymore came into possession of the Hamilton family, having been inherited by Ellen Magennis, wife of William Hamilton. It passed to their son James, and when he died in 1701, it passed to his son, also James, who was created Lord Limerick in 1719. Around 1720, a hunting lodge seems to have been built, and it was probably then that the estate was enclosed to form a Deer Park.

James began the construction of a grander house around 1750 in what is now the lower carpark. He was advised by Thomas Wright, an English architect, astronomer and mathematician, who had visited Tollymore in 1746. James also established an arboretum to the west of the house, and constructed the Old Bridge (1726) and Clanbrassil Barn (1757).[31]

On his death in 1758, Tollymore was inherited by his son, also James. He greatly enlarged the house, and continued the programme of tree planting begun by his father. Over a twelve year period in the 1770s, and '80s, he planted no less than a third of a million trees to the north of the Drinns. In the 1780s he also erected the Barbican Gate (1780), Ivy Bridge (1780), Foley's Bridge (1787), Bryansford Gate (1786), the Hermitage, Parnell's Bridge, and the Follies on the Hilltown Road. Again, many of their features were inspired by Wright's earlier work.

James died without issue in 1798 and the property passed to his sister Anne, Countess of Roden whose husband Robert Jocelyn, the first Earl, had died the year before. This connection with the Rodens was to endure for almost 150 years.

During the 1800s, the demesne was renowned for its 'naturalistic' landscape, and by the time of Green's visits, the public were allowed in on a regular basis. The commercial potential of the woodland was also recognized with the opening by the 3rd Earl of a water-powered sawmill near Foley's Bridge in 1828; two small ponds and a lengthy millrace mark its site.

In 1930, Robert, the 8th Earl, sold two-thirds of the estate to the Ministry of Agriculture for tree planting. The remaining land, mostly on the north bank of the Shimna, was bought up in 1941.

The demesne re-opened as Northern Ireland's first Forest Park in 1955. Although still a commercial forest, producing some 2000 tons of timber annually, it is also used for many recreational activities: walking, camping, caravaning, horse riding and orienteering. The Northern Ireland Mountain Centre also occupies part of the estate on the Hilltown Road.

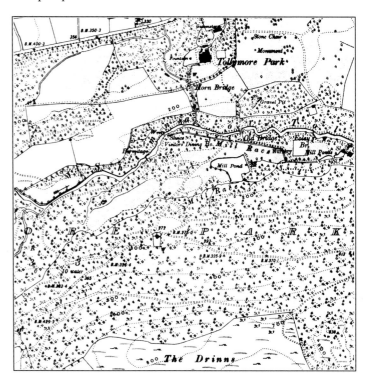

TOLLYMORE HOUSE, 1920 (Ordnance Survey)

TOLLYMORE HOUSE (WAG 564)

The house was begun by James Hamilton, 1st Lord Limerick, around 1750, and greatly enlarged by his son in the later 1700s. During World War II, American troops were stationed here. The house afterwards fell into disrepair and was demolished in 1952. The lower carpark now marks its site.

FOLEY'S BRIDGE, TOLLYMORE (WAG 565)

The Shimna River (known as the Hanolock in the 1700s) cuts through the demesne from west to east. Across it are a number of small bridges including this hump-backed footbridge over a rocky chasm. A datestone records its construction by the 2nd Lord Limerick in 1787. It commemorates his marriage to Grace Foley, as indicated by a second stone inscribed *Ht : Foley*. Note also the baps (*cf.* page 83).

BRYANSFORD GATE, TOLLYMORE (WAG 1)

This buttressed granite arch, now the Forest Park exit, was erected by the 2nd Lord Limerick in 1786. It is quite different in style to the Barbican Gate built around the same time (and now the park entrance). The Rodens opened Tollymore to the public, the two signs informing visitors of the opening hours on Tuesdays and Fridays. Unlike today no dogs, horses or motor cars were then allowed. Behind, a tree-lined avenue leads down to the Clanbrassil Barn.

RODEN ARMS, BRYANSFORD (WAG 563)
Still retaining much of its character as an estate village, many of Bryansford's houses date to the late 1700s and early 1800s. Sadly for Green, the inn was no longer in use, having closed when the Slieve Donard Hotel opened in 1898. A fenced mall opposite served as a promenade for guests, who were also allowed into the demesne. The inn's protecting gables, left of centre, have since been removed although the Mall is still maintained.

UNUSED PHOTOGRAPHS

Whilst we have endeavoured to show a representative selective of Green's photographs, many must remain unused. These are listed below by catalogue number, all of which are prefixed by 'WAG'. They may be viewed, by appointment, in the library of the Ulster Folk & Transport Museum.

1A	Gothic Gate, Tollymore	590	Christ Church, Kilkeel	2601	Mournes from north
2	Ivy Bridge, Tollymore	595	Greencastle St, Kilkeel	2602	Mournes from north
3	Newcastle	597	Kilkeel Harbour	2604	Shimna River, Newcastle
4	Seafront, Newcastle	1436	Tullybrannigan Bridge	2606	Mournes from Newcastle
4A	Seafront, Newcastle	1437	Tullybrannigan Bridge	2607	Mournes from north
5	Newcastle from north	1439	Shimna River, Newcastle	2608	Newcastle from north
12	Clonachullion Bridge	1440	Mournes from north	2609	Mournes from Newcastle
13	Clonachullion Bridge	1442	Newcastle from south	2610	Upper Shimna Valley
33	Seafront, Newcastle	1699	Golf clubhouse, Newcastle	2612	Trassey Track
34	Promenade, Newcastle	1702	Slieve Bingian	2612A	Trassey Track
38	Roden Arms, Bryansford	1703	Slieve Bingian	2614	Promenade, Newcastle
47	The castle, Greencastle	1704	Silent Valley	2615	Promenade, Newcastle
551	Sl. Donard Hotel, Newcastle	1705	Kilkeel-Hilltown road	2618	Golf clubhouse, Newcastle
552	Sl. Donard Hotel, Newcastle	1707	River Bann, Hilltown	2621	Glen River, Newcastle
553	Golf clubhouse, Newcastle	1708	Mountain farm	2622	Glen River, Newcastle
554	Main St, Newcastle	1714	Mournes from north	2623	Mournes from north
555	Main St, Newcastle	1715	Mournes from north	2624	The Mall, Bryansford
556	Main St, Newcastle	1716	Lough Shannagh	2626	Mournes from north
557	Main St, Newcastle	1718	Kilkeel River, Kilkeel	2631	Carginagh Road, Kilkeel
558	Seafront, Newcastle	1719	Mournes from north	2654	Newcastle from north
568	Glen River, Newcastle	1721	Kilkeel Harbour	2661	Slieve Bingian
569	Glen River, Newcastle	1722	Kilkeel Harbour	2662	Slieve Bingian
570	Glen River, Newcastle	1782	Cranfield Bay	2662A	Slieve Bingian
572	Mournes from Newcastle	1887	Cassy Water	2666	Upper Shimna Valley
574	Cock and Hen mountains	1887A	Cassy Water	2667	Shimna Bridges, Newcastle
575	Clonachullion Bridge	1859	Barbican Gate, Tollymore	2667A	Shimna Bridges, Newcastle
579	Glen River, Newcastle	1984	Wooden plough	2673	Mournes from south
580	Glen River, Newcastle	2037	Cassy Water	2676	Annalong River
586	Silent Valley	2056	The castle, Greencastle	2677A	Kilkeel Harbour
589	Crawtree Stone, Kilkeel	2214	Hare's Gap	2678	Cottage, Kilkeel

2679	Cottage, Kilkeel	3062B	Cock and Hen mountains	3437	Donard Lodge, Newcastle
2680A	Kilkeel beach	3064	Spence's Bridge, Glasdrumman	3438	Donard Lodge, Newcastle
2681	Kilkeel beach	3065	Trassey River	3439	Donard Lodge, Newcastle
2682	Kilkeel Harbour	3066	Mournes from west	3495	Shimna River
2682A	Kilkeel Harbour	3081	Bloody Bridge	3497	Annalong Valley
2684A	Mourne Park	3082	Kilkeel Harbour	3571	Silent Valley
2685A	Old Bridge, Mourne Park	3083	Trassey River	3590	Glasdrumman beach
2686	The castle, Greencastle	3084	Mountain farm	3604	Tor, Slieve Commedagh
2689	Silent Valley	3085	Slieve Bingian		
2690	Slieve Bingian	3088	Newcastle from north		
2695	Kilkeel-Hilltown road	3090	Annalong Harbour		
2696	Cottage, Kilkeel	3091	Promenade, Newcastle		
2715	Cassy Water	3093	Mournes from north		
2715A	Cassy Water	3095	Mournes from north		
2716	Cassy Water	3098	Foffany		
2716A	Cassy Water Bridge	3099	Foffany		
2717	White Water River	3110	Sl. Donard Hotel, Newcastle		
2719	Mournes from south	3111	Sl. Donard Hotel, Newcastle		
2720A	Newcastle Road, Annalong	3113	Sl. Donard Hotel, Newcastle		
2721	Cornmill, Annalong Harbour	3114	Golf clubhouse, Newcastle		
2723	Newcastle Harbour	3116	Promenade, Newcastle		
2738	Hare's Gap	3117	Promenade, Newcastle		
2739	Boat House, Mourne Park	3118	Newcastle from north		
2740	Kilkeel-Hilltown road	3119	Newcastle from north		
2750	Silent Valley Reservoir	3120	Main St, Newcastle		
2988	Silent Valley Reservoir	3121	Main St, Newcastle		
2989	Slieve Bingian	3122	Main St, Newcastle		
2990	Mourne Park	3224	Mournes from south		
2991	Mournes from west	3284	Smokery, Kilkeel Harbour		
2992	Tea-rooms, Manse Rd, Kilkeel	3293	Kilkeel Harbour		
2994	Tea-rooms, Manse Rd, Kilkeel	3341	Spelga Pass		
3055	Foffany	3365	Kilkeel Harbour		
3057	Mournes from west	3366	Fishing boat		
3059	Clonachullion Bridge	3383	Annalong Harbour		
3061	Hen Mountain	3393	Kilkeel Harbour		
3062A	Cock and Hen mountains	3413	Cranfield beach		

REFERENCES

1. K.R. Hirons, 'The changing vegetation of the Mournes', *12 miles of Mourne*, **2** (1988): 43-51.
2. A. Sheridan, 'A newly-discovered prehistoric site at Annalong, and its archaeological background', in T. Steele and P. Robinson (eds) *Field excursions in Ulster, Vol.3 - The Annalong district of the Mournes, County Down*: 2-9 (Cultra: Ulster Folklife Society, 1985).
3. A. Sheridan, 'Early settlers of Mourne', *12 miles*, **3** (1989): 12-25.
4. T. Porter, 'Mourne surnames', *12 miles*, **3** (1989): 57-62.
5. C. Elizabeth, 'A walk on the wild side', *12 miles*, **3** (1989): 52-56.
6. M. Fearon, '19th century impressions of Mourne', *12 miles*, **3** (1989): 26-32.
7. Unfortunately much of the subject matter, coupled with the slow pace of change, makes it impossible to date precisely many of the photographs.
8. A fuller discussion of Newcastle's development is to be found in G. Morton, *Victorian and Edwardian Newcastle* (Belfast: Friar's Bush Press, 1988). A town trail is described in *Walk about Newcastle* (Downpatrick: Down Museum, 1986).
9. E.M. Patterson, *The Belfast & Co.Down Railway* (Newton Abbot: David & Charles, 1982).
10. H. McCaw and B. Henderson, *The Royal Co.Down Golf Club: the first century* (Belfast: Universities Press, 1988).
11. There is ongoing debate as to where French wrote these lines, but he was most likely inspired when walking on the beach at Skerries, just north of Dublin.
12. Walter Harris in *The Antient and Present State of the County of Down* (1744) gives a particularly vivid account of these events.
13. Rev. J. O'Laverty, *A Historical account of the Diocese of Down and Connor, ancient and modern, Vol.1* (Dublin: Duffy, 1878; reprinted by Davidson Books, Spa, 1980).
14. The development of the port is summarized by M. McCaughan, 'Nineteenth century accounts of maritime activity at Annalong', *Field excursions*: 24-35.
15. Hand dressing of granite boulders is described by T. Steele, 'Stonemen', *Field excursions*: 69-73.
16. Skiff fishing is detailed by E. McBride and A. Kilgore in *Field excursions*: 35-42; and by H. Allen, 'At sea with the Annalong skiffs', *12 miles*, **4** (1991): 48.
17. F. Hamond, 'The restoration of Annalong cornmill', *Field excursions*: 21-24.
18. For a fuller discussion of traditional Mourne settlement, see articles by P. Robinson, T. Steele and D. Nicholson in *Field excursions*: 44-57.
19. J. Bell, 'Wooden ploughs from Mourne', *Field excursions*: 63-65.
20. T. Bradshaw, *The general directory of Newry, Armagh and other towns for 1820* (Newry, Wilkinson, 1819; reprinted by Davidson Books, Spa, 1984).
21. For a profile of Kilkeel at this time, see D. Moorehead and V. Stevenson, 'Kilkeel in the 1830s', *12 miles*, **2** (1988): 54-63.
22. M. Fearon and F. MacCann, 'Kilkeel workhouse', *12 Miles*, **1** (1987): 32-44.
23. The town's commercial evolution is outlined by B. and C. Hudson, 'Changing commerce in Kilkeel', *12 miles*, **2** (1988): 21-28.
24. Schooner operations are analysed by H. Irvine, 'Mourne coaster sailing operations in 1900-01', *12 miles*, **1** (1987): 62-74. Detailed appraisals of the fishing industry are also given by M. McCaughan and V. Pollock in M. McCaughan and J. Appleby (eds) *The Irish Sea: aspects of maritime history*: 120-144 (Belfast: Institute of Irish Studies, Queen's University, and Cultra: Ulster Folk and Transport Museum, 1989).
25. Chesney's extraordinary life is recounted by T. Porter, 'General F.R. Chesney', *12 miles*, **4** (1991): 27-33.
26. L. Murphy, 'Action stations: the story of Greencastle Aerodrome', *12 Miles*, **3** (1989): 33-50.
27. Some idea of the complexity of dividing up in-blown wrack is given by S. Nicholson, 'Dividing the wrack on Derryogue shore in the '30s', *12 miles*, **1** (1987): 60.
28. The development of the Mourne water supply is detailed in J. Loudan, *In search of water* (Belfast: Belfast City & District Water Commissioners, 1940).
29. The building of the dam is vividly described by W.H. Carson, *The dam builders* (Newcastle: Mourne Observer Press, 1981).
30. F. Hamond, 'The Lough Shannagh Pumped Storage Scheme', *12 miles*, **3** (1989): 63-66.
31. Fuller details of many of the estate's features are given in *Tollymore Forest Park*, produced by the Forest Service of the Dept. Agriculture (Belfast: HMSO, 1981).

SELECT GENERAL BIBLIOGRAPHY

Virtually every topic touched upon in this book is covered by the late Estyn Evans in his seminal work *Mourne country* (Dundalk: Dundalgan Press, 1951, revised 1967).

The late Joe Doran also published widely on life in Mourne: *Hill walks in the Mournes* (Newcastle: Mourne Observer Press, 1973); *My Mourne* (Newcastle: Mourne Observer Press, 1974); *Wayfarer in Mourne* (Rathfriland: Outlook Press, 1980); *Turn up the lamp* (Belfast: Appletree Press, 1980).

An overview of Mourne in the 1830s is given in the Ordnance Survey Memoirs. These have been edited by A. Day and P. McWilliams, and reprinted as *Ordnance Survey memoirs of Ireland - Parishes of Co.Down* I, 1834-6: South Down (Belfast: Institute of Irish Studies, Queen's University, Belfast, 1990).

Descriptions of many of the area's fine buildings are in P.J. Rankin, *Historic buildings in the Mourne area of South Down* (Belfast: Ulster Architectural Heritage Society, 1975).

Recent events, as recorded in the Newcastle-based Mourne Observer, have been indexed by J. McCoy, *An index to the Mourne Observer, 1949-1980* (Ballynahinch: South-Eastern Education and Library Board). The Library has also produced *The Mournes: A source list* (1984).

Many aspects of Mourne are featured in *12 miles of Mourne*, Journal of the Kilkeel-based Mourne Local Studies Group.

ACKNOWLEDGEMENTS

Besides the numerous authors cited above, we are grateful to many people for information supplied: the librarian and staff of Newcastle and Ballynahinch Libraries, James Baird, Johnathan Bell, Archie Cairns, Wilfred Capper, Hal and Sharon Dawson, Arthur Doran, Diane Forbes, Robbie Graham, George Hanna, David Johnson, Fred Johnston, Elizabeth McBride, John Mackintosh, John Moore, Herbie Morrison, Jack and Ivy Newell, Victor Neill, Alec Robinson, and Richard Warner. Margaret McNulty and Brian Walker of Friar's Bush Press made many helpful suggestions. Thanks are also due to Trustees of the Ulster Folk & Transport Museum for permission to reproduce the Green photographs. We are especially indebted to Ken Anderson and his staff for supplying such high-quality prints.